Through gates of un₁
a thousand welcomes.

In this eloquent, yet bold collection you find a wide variety from formal sestinas and sonnets to free verse. Poems herein encompass the realms of Lovecraft's dark gothic to Schwader's take on science and the stars. The haibun are outstanding, with lines such as these from "Alien Machines": "We are / besieged, our dreams bled out upon strange altars." I've been a fan of Ann Schwader since I first laid eyes on sf poetry in the 80's, and will never part with her collections, each as precious as the next. Ann's work is superlative.

Marge Simon, multiple Bram Stoker Award® winner

Ann truly continues in her course of producing dark, menacing poetry executed in meticulous, masterly strophes. She's far too accomplished in the art ever to be considered nowadays as a Poet Laureate.

Richard L. Tierney, author *Savage Menace*

I've been enjoying and admiring Ann Schwader's poetry for nearly thirty years. Her work ranges from Lovecraftian re-inventions to science fictional visions, from strict metric forms to free verse, and is always expertly crafted. Rich in imagination, in emotions and ideas, *Dark Energies* is a collection that any devotee of genre poetry will savor.

Bruce Boston, SFPA Grandmaster

Ann Schwader's precise metrical skills and phantasmagorical imagination have made her what has been described as one of the four leading Lovecraftian Mythos poets in the world. She is as skilled a prose writer as she is a poet, and will be remembered as one of the leading poets of our time.

Fred Phillips, author *From the Cauldron*

Ann K. Schwader (long one of our foremost poets of the weird and the speculative), here in this brand new collection demonstrates her versatility with form as well as with subject matter. These verses range from homages to some of the giants of the weird field (Clark Ashton Smith, Robert W. Chambers, H. P. Lovecraft), to poems imbued with her love of ancient civilisations, to poignant and philosophical meditations on various states of being. Schwader excels at verse evoking with deft precision the dark energies that permeate the universe, including the myth and legend of earth's hidden corners. This new volume will only enhance her reputation as a poet of stirring depth and wicked imagination.

Leigh Blackmore, author *Spores from Sharnoth*

Look no further than Schwader's new collection for exquisite evocations of the macabre. To works like "Eating Mummy," "Lullaby for Arachnophobes" and the "Keziah" sonnet cycle, she brings not only her consummate craft but a livid intensity, a wicked wit, and the possibility that the horrors of the outer dark might be preferable to our own paradoxical inhumanity.

Kyla Lee Ward, author *The Land of Bad Dreams*

This volume can only leave readers thirsting for more poetic jewels from her pen.

S. T. Joshi, author *I Am Providence*

Ann Schwader does with "mere" words, magic indeed.

Robert M. Price, author *Blasphemies and Revelations*

Dark Energies

Dark Energies

Ann K. Schwader

With a Preface by S. T. Joshi
and an Afterword by Robert M. Price

Edited by Charles Lovecraft

P'REA PRESS

Sydney, Australia

2015

Ann K. Schwader lives and writes in Colorado. Her most recent collection is *Dark Equinox and Other Tales of Lovecraftian Horror* (Hippocampus Press, 2015). Her *Wild Hunt of the Stars* (Sam's Dot, 2010) was a Bram Stoker Award finalist. She is also a 2010 Rhysling Award winner and the Poet Laureate for NecronomiCon Providence 2015.

P'rea Press, Sydney, Australia, www.preapress.com
First edition, August 2015.

Cover and illustrations © by David Schembri Studios 2015.
Preface © by S. T. Joshi 2015.
Afterword © by Robert M. Price 2015.
Cover and illustrations designed by David Schembri Studios.
Publisher's logo designed by Charles Lovecraft.
Book designed by David E. Schultz.
Set in Adobe Caslon Pro type 11 point.
Printed by Lightning Source through various locations worldwide.

National Library of Australia Cataloguing-in-Publication
Creator: Schwader, Ann K., author.
Title: Dark energies / Ann K. Schwader; S. T. Joshi; Robert M. Price; Charles Lovecraft.
ISBN: 9780980462517 (paperback)
Notes: Includes bibliographical references.
Subjects: American poetry.
Other Creators/Contributors:
Joshi, S. T., 1958– writer of preface.
Price, Robert M., 1954– writer of afterword.
Lovecraft, Charles, 1955– editor.
Dewey Number: 811.54

For S. T. W.

in friendship & memory

Contents

Preface

The emergence, over the past two or three decades, of Ann K. Schwader as perhaps the leading weird poet of our time has been steady and sure. From *The Worms Remember* (2001) to *Architectures of Night* (2003) to *In the Yaddith Time* (2007) to *Wild Hunt of the Stars* (2010), Schwader has exhibited a mastery of poetic technique and an imaginative richness that have placed her at the pinnacle of her field. *Twisted in Dream: The Collected Weird Poetry of Ann K. Schwader* (2011) seemed a fitting capstone to her achievement; but she is not content to rest on her laurels, as triumphantly demonstrated in this new book of scintillating lyrics.

It is a good time to be a poet of fantasy, terror, and the supernatural. No one can deny that a genuine renaissance in this long-neglected subgenre is taking place. During the heyday of *Weird Tales* in the 1920s and 1930s, poets such as Clark Ashton Smith, H. P. Lovecraft, Robert E. Howard, Donald Wandrei, and Frank Belknap Long made lasting contributions to the form; but in the succeeding decades, only such relatively lonely figures as Richard L. Tierney, Joseph Payne Brennan and Stanley McNail added to it. In recent decades, however, we have seen such poets as Leigh Blackmore, Wade German, Michael Fantina, Fred Phillips, and Charles Lovecraft (who skilfully fills the double role of poet and publisher) come to the fore. Several publishers regularly issue substantial books of weird poetry, and magazines such as *Spectral Realms* are exclusively devoted to the form.

What sets Schwader's work apart from that of her contemporaries is not merely her impeccable poetic technique—she has demonstrated conclusively that formal verse is far and away superior to free verse in the capturing of concentrated images of horror and strangeness—but in a kind of cosmic pessimism that makes her poems far more than mere exercises in shudder-coining. The imperishable lines from "A Voyage(r) Too Far"—"Humanity, / Beyond the fragile light that marks our star, / May prove no more than fireflies in a jar / Against the mindless void"—captures the essence of that vision. Possibly it is a vision partly derived from the work of Smith or Lovecraft; but it is too heartfelt, and expressed in too personal and intense a manner, to be merely the product of literary influence.

This is not to deny that there are literary influences on Schwader's poetry. This book contains numerous poems that derive from—or, perhaps more accurately, engage in a vibrant and constructive imaginative dialogue with—the writings of Smith, Lovecraft, Robert W. Chambers, Edgar Allan Poe, and so many other leading writers of weird fiction. How far Schwader is from mechanical pastiche can be seen in a poem like "Climate of Fear," an extraordinarily compact encapsulation of the essence of Lovecraft's Antarctic novella *At the Mountains of Madness*. Lovecraft, indeed, may be a dominant influence, or, at any rate, a dominant figure with whom Schwader wishes to engage: "Keziah" is a moving sonnet cycle that focuses on the central figure in "The Dreams in the Witch House," probing the depths of that cosmic witch's mind and psyche in a way that Lovecraft himself could not bring himself to do. And even such recent writers as W. H. Pugmire and the late lamented Adam Niswander come in for poignant poetical tributes.

It would be an error to think that cosmic terror is the sole focus of Schwader's poetry. Her imaginative palette is remarkably wide, and such a poem as "Giving Up the Ghost," with its striking opening line ("It's habit-forming, being haunted"), exhibits a grim whimsicality that other poems in this book build upon. And in terms of form, we find here a brace of exquisite prose-poems (with an admixture of haiku-like poetic fragments) that make it abundantly clear that Schwader can do far more than write flawless sonnets and quatrains. (Indeed, her prose fiction is now gaining an ever-increasing following, as her recent volume *Dark Equinox and Other Tales of Lovecraftian Horror* [2015] demonstrates.)

We have certainly not heard the last of Ann K. Schwader, and this volume can only leave readers thirsting for more poetic jewels from her pen. What further work will emerge in the coming years and decades it is impossible to predict; but it is safe to say that every poem will embody the technical perfection, the meticulous care in word-choice, the imaginative range, and the brooding sense of humanity's fragile and transient place in the universe that we find throughout this book. It is, as I say, a good time to be a weird poet; but it is an even better time to be a reader of weird poetry.

—S. T. JOSHI

Seattle, Washington
June 2015

"Into That Darkness Peering . . ."
An Interview with Ann K. Schwader

by Charles Lovecraft, July 2015

To date how many of your poems are published? Has it reached a thousand ?

No, I really don't know at this point. It might be as high as a thousand, but I'm guessing more like 800. If you include the mainstream haiku I've been writing & seeing published in journals for the past decade or so, definitely at least 800.

Is Dark Energies *your first Australian publication?*

I'm not sure this counts as my first publication in Australia. I had work in the February 2011 issue of *Midnight Echo*, the magazine of the Australian Horror Writers Association. This consisted of two poems: "The Quiet One," & "The Dead Come Back." Both were reprinted in *Twisted in Dream*. However, it's definitely my first book / collection to be published in Australia.

In Wild Hunt of the Stars and now Dark Energies, I perceive a distancing from pure horror and a tendency towards social critique. Some of the poems seem to ask questions about life, meaning and existence, and to question human attitudes. The poems "Time Ghosts" and "Towers of Light" in Dark Energies, for instance, seem to comment socially and to exhibit a sense of modernity. Do you feel that your poetry is evolving into a deeper social consciousness and perhaps mainstream position?

Wild Hunt of the Stars and *Dark Energies* both contain a good bit of dark SF poetry, as opposed to what you call "pure horror." As Lovecraftians know, horror and SF aren't mutually exclusive, and in fact play very nicely together. Dark SF just brings in different horrors

to add to the mix—like the nuclear winter in "Towers of Light."
"Time Ghosts" comes from another one of my favorite inspirations,
history. History has all the horror anyone could ask for, because it's
made by humans. Unfortunately—or maybe fortunately—they're not
very imaginative. The same awful behavior patterns tend to repeat
through the centuries, with a varied cast of characters. Being a news
junkie hasn't helped my view of this, either.

I don't see my poetry as trying for a deeper social consciousness
so much as trying to find new & interesting subject matter. I've been
writing weird verse (among other types) for almost three decades
now, and I want to keep bringing something fresh to the party. I'm a
traditionalist / formalist when it comes to structuring my poems, but
I don't see why traditional techniques can't be used to craft weird
verse from more contemporary materials.

To my way of thinking (and I am not a literary critic!), the weird
involves trying to suggest what can't be figured out—the unknown
and unknowable. Despite the best efforts of science, we don't seem
to be running out of things we don't know & possibly can't know.
Thus, a weird approach to poetry should keep right on working into
modernity.

*As I recall, there was a feeling you expressed once or twice in emails to me
about "feminine perspective." You mentioned "Lavinia" and feminist
concerns in literature. Please tell us more about this.*

I think I may have said something about wanting to bring a
feminine (or just female) perspective to Lovecraftian writing,
actually. I've heard people complain that Lovecraft didn't do much
with his female characters, or didn't do them very well. This may be
true, but there's nothing to keep other writers from revisiting those
characters and doing more with them. I've done this more in my
fiction than my poetry, but in the past few years I've also done
narrative sonnet sequences for Lavinia Whateley and Keziah Mason.
These may strike readers as revisionist, but I was careful to reread the

tales themselves and not change the essential plot points. Lavinia and Keziah become the heroines (or anti-heroine, in Keziah's case) of their own narratives, and I concern myself with *their* motives and goals. Hopefully, this makes for an entertaining reading experience!

I've also found inspiration in some of Lovecraft's less-developed entities. Mother Hydra hasn't gotten nearly the press Father Dagon has, and it's interesting to do something about that. It's also reflective of older mythologies, since many of them (those I've read about, anyhow) did have goddesses with significant power. Why not give Deep Ones a Great Mother of their own? Then there are Lovecraft's ghouls—he made them canine, but I've always wondered why they couldn't have been hyena-based. Better jaws for breaking bones, better tolerance for very "high" protein sources . . . and, of course, hyenas are matriarchal. Matriarchal ghouls are just plain fun to write about, though I'm certain I'm not the only woman writer in the Mythos who does them. I've also created my own female Lovecraftian entity, Ammutseba, though I think she's gotten maybe two or three poems and a short story so far.

I'm honestly not sure whether being a feminist—and I can't remember when I wasn't one—affects how I write dark poetry. It probably doesn't influence my cosmic horror much, since the whole point of that is revealing humanity as flies on the galactic windshield. Whether those flies are male or female doesn't matter to the dark presences of the Void, or that asteroid with all our names on it out there somewhere. It probably does affect my other dark poetry. I really don't like showing women as victims, and I love finding women in mythology and writing about them.

Speaking of poetry and the "mainstream," have you written specifically to suit non-genre publications; or did you send some of your weird poems to them; or both?

I used to submit work to a mainstream magazine called *The Formalist,* but that one's gone now (sadly), and I don't really make an effort to send work to mainstream publications other than haiku journals. I've had a little bit of success with my mainstream haiku—i.e., I've had work in a couple of important anthologies in addition to the better journals—but some of those haiku were still pretty dark! My personal favorite—and the one that's done the best in terms of being reprinted—is a hairline away from horror.

I think that after a while, you tend to bring your "dark mind" or "spec mind" [speculative mind] with you to whatever you write. Some mainstream editors can accept this and some can't. Mainstream English-language haiku generally seems to be open to a thread of imagination running through. It just has to be subtle.

If you're curious about which haiku anthologies & journals I've been in, that info is on my website on the biography page.

What is your perspective on mainstream poetry and "imaginative poetry," as independent literary expressions? You could elaborate on your poetic tastes, the poets and styles you have read and like, perhaps even the greatest influences upon yourself and your work.

I can't say that I've ever seen imaginative poetry as independent from other poetry. Isn't all good poetry imaginative? Genre poems or speculative poems or whatever else you want to call poems that put the unreal front & center are just a subset of the larger set Poetry. And, like all other poems, they need to be well-crafted as well as well-imagined in order to be effective. Good speculative poems may be harder to write than good mainstream poems, though, because they do need that extra dose of wonder.

Most important poetic influences? Edna St. Vincent Millay, though she's not a weird poet (aside from at least one brief poem, "Humoresque," which is absolutely chilling). She also isn't much read any more, but I discovered her as a teen. She has a long sonnet sequence, *Fatal Interview*, that I couldn't stop reading. It's romantic and dark and very well-constructed, and I knew I wanted to write sonnets after that. I also learned from her work how effective rhyme and meter could be, though it took me a very long time to come back to that realization. Shakespeare showed me why iambic pentameter is a Wonderful Thing, but he wasn't the one who made me want to try it for myself.

I know I ought to mention Poe, but I haven't read enough of his poetry recently to comment. I also haven't read nearly enough of the other classic weird poets, though I keep trying to remedy this deficit. I think my favorite of these so far is Clark Ashton Smith, though I've got to take his poetry in small doses. Too much at once tends to overwhelm the mind.

Dark Energies

Void Flyers

Vibrating night, a violence of wings
Disturbs the minds of some few sensitive
Enough to pierce mere matter, & forgive
All limits of imagination. Things
Are not as our eyes lie to us in this
Dim corner of a dying universe:
The energies of darkness laid their curse
Upon it from the start, for what exists
Reveals itself in glimpses of a whole
Our senses cannot hope to contemplate
This side of sanity—nor explicate
Without some fatal stain upon the soul.

These unseen flyers at the fringe of sleep,
Whose shadow-wings beat outward at a pace
Increasing every moment, murder space
Itself with their black passage. Thus they keep
Strange faith with entities of elder void,
Who cry like ravens at spacetime destroyed.

In This Brief Interval

Before our sun first sparked, the stars turned right
Beyond some liminal apocalypse
To herald the return of elder night.

Sunk deep in ignorance we name delight,
Such cosmic truth will never stain our lips:
Before our sun first sparked, the stars turned right.

One Arab mystic dared describe that sight
Before he suffered sanity's eclipse
To herald the return of elder night.

What matter all the rockets we ignite
To launch sleek probes or long-range sleeper ships?
Before our sun first sparked, the stars turned right.

Mundane events monopolize our fright,
Obscuring time's frail fabric as it rips
To herald the return of elder night.

Dizzied by ascension to this height,
We never feel it when the balance tips.
Before our sun first sparked, the stars turned right
To herald the return of elder night.

Cordyceps zombii

They glittered mystery in the desert night,
those sparks from space we came to know as spores
but saw at first by childhood's light: each mind
its own myth-maker. So contagion spread
as evils always have, without intent
beyond some impulse to perfect one's life.

Humanity's quixotic quest for life
outside our homeworld orbit stopped that night
successfully. Forever. By intent
or otherwise, our fate lay with those spores
drawn deeper with each sleeping breath to spread
their threads of hunger & ensnare the mind.

Why did the notion never come to mind
that loneliness was safer? Surely life
elsewhere might have its own agenda, spread
itself upon the star-winds until night
exploded with new constellations: spores
enough for legions linked by one intent.

Unceasing motion seemed the sole intent
sustaining the infested. Maimed in mind,
they roved as little more than meat for spores
of future generations. Aping life
no longer theirs, these shamblers by night
soon burst with fruiting death as terror spread.

From continent to continent the spread
accelerated, fueled by good intent
turned tragic as a shotgun in the night
unthinkingly deployed. Each spattered mind
released in turn its epitaph to life
as we once lived it, innocent of spores.

Adrift in this necropolis where spores
abandoned us at last, survivors spread
a thousand warning satellites for life
which might approach our planet. Yet intent
undoes us still: each thread-infested mind
cries out in siren welcome to the night.

So life perfects its own malign intent
until the stars are merely spores which spread
in mindless currents to the curve of night.

Alien Machines

No one sleeps by night in our neighborhood. The din starts long past sunset, wrenching heads from pillows with the unnatural deaths of steel and concrete, the eradication of landmarks. Warning shrieks mark juggernauts flailing to their own rhythms in darkness. None of this is of our world. We are besieged, our dreams bled out upon strange altars.

> cracked pane
> a shattering
> of stars

First light reveals mud and wreckage. The ravaged skeleton of an old bridge, long marked for replacement. Pallid filaments of that replacement quiver on either side of a fresh abyss. The drying earth is scarified by tracks: cuneiform script in a language our tongues cannot form. Whatever made them has gone elsewhere.

> the cave mouth's
> event horizon
> breath

Our complaints to the city fathers are duly ignored. Construction was ordered and funded, construction progresses on its own schedule. If the ends of this new bridge show no sign of meeting—if they claw upward for the stars—why is that our concern?

Only that bridges stretch both ways.

> moonrise
> one constellation
> out of place

Fatal Constellations

Only dark is real: the stars
are brittle, transitory things
already lost. Their myths like scars
across the face of night may bring
some temporary order, fling
a bone to reason . . . but the rest
& most is chaos ravening
past sight. Our elemental quest
for pictures in the Great Rift tests
such limitations, tracing shapes
of void from starlight till we wrest
significance—if not escape—
from ignorance. Yet is it wise
to seek the Real that shuns disguise?

Deconstructing Night

Demolish first the false dichotomy
of clotted darkness threatening moonlight.
That one is sane & holy in our sight,
the other neither, merely seems to be
(on close analysis) a privileged view
of questionable worth. This shadowed text
might shelter its fair share of terrors, true;
but who are you to say so? Might the next
dark angel's radically alternative
perspective not apply as well? Efface
hierarchical assumptions, & embrace
that arbitrary madness which still lives
between these penciled lines of dusk & dawn—
the last postmodern haunt of chaos-spawn.

The Laundrymen

They trundle through the gaslit London night
With overburdened carts whose banshee wheels
Cry havoc through the poorest districts. Flight
Is fruitless here, & even sleep to heal
Life's lighter wounds comes seldom. When it seals
Dim eyes forever, little can be done
By way of mourning. Better not to feel
Too much beyond hard currency from one
Who offers. Takes. The grim charade's begun
Once more, soiled linen bundled high to mask
Still-cooling meat from conscience. With the sun
So far from rising, better not to ask
Exactly *which* anatomist awaits . . .
Or why this silent minion salivates.

Necropolis Railway Incident

The trains that run all night beneath the dreams
of London rumble heavy with the dead
long exiled into memory & weeds
entangled. Decades past their final breath,
phantasms of a vanished scheme still drift
between Brookwood & Waterloo, unfazed
by tracks reduced to shadow, or the Blitz
that razed their chapel terminus. No day
of judgment threatens: sorted First to Third
already & forever, they defy
all lesser magistrates to do their worst
against a fate so tastefully applied.

Yet sometimes in their passage through this dark
carved into elder darkness, lights appear
from lives still whirling, glittering & hard
as stars. Or signals. Eager, unsecured
by parcels or valises, they descend
with yellowed tickets & unknown intent.

Giving Up the Ghost

It's habit-forming, being haunted. Nights
just aren't the same without that dragging chain
like Marley on your stairs, or some refrain
of wailing in the rafters. Mundane frights
fall short of *frisson* when such rare delights
as these abide, reminding us how pain
or longing long years ended may sustain
itself by shadows at the edge of sight.

But haunts aren't modern. No one has the time
for spectral frivols now, so it seems best
to go cold raven: just refuse to host
more paranormal boarders. In their prime,
their company was hardly worth your rest;
so little's lost by giving up the ghost.

Thoughts At the Passing Bell

What they might say when I am dead,
I cannot hope to alter, no,
& so vile tongues are comforted.
What they might say when I am dead
Must stand . . . unless, as I once read,
Wronged spirits slip this planet slow.
What they might say when I am dead,
I cannot hope to alter? *No.*

Mercy, Mercy

None called her heartless while she lived,
& yet her specter roams about
on Chestnut Hill some winter nights
with breastbone leaking stars. No doubt

her neighbors meant well. To demand
three exhumations—& the last
a sanguine horror—argues minds
so blinded by a pagan past

as to be nearly innocent
of what transpired. Strange sacrifice
to offer in this Christian place:
a maiden's heart to meet the price

of brother's life. Perhaps he died
still tasting ashes two months hence,
& knowing them for hers. Perhaps
he lacked the local confidence

in vampires & their cure. Though that's
mere speculation, history
will always fall to dust against
the sweeter meat of mystery

on Chestnut Hill. Some winter nights,
a weathered bridge which spans the flood
of ice there hosts a deeper chill . . .
her scent of roses, sweet as blood.

—in memoriam Mercy Lena Brown, d. 1892

A Maid Betray'd

Weep with me, willow
That grows by my door;
My love loves another . . .
(It's happened before.)

Sigh with me, bluebells
So faithful & true;
He tried to deny
What I already knew.

Mystical moonbeams
That shone on our kissing,
Let him not notice
His razor is missing.

Gentle night breezes
That whispered of dreaming,
Send me a high wind
To drown out his screaming.

Lavinia in Autumn

(Sentinel Hill)

Ancestral echoes from these hilltop stones
Erected by no hands the living know
Call shadows out of autumn: those below,
Who sated darkness with their blood & bone.
Such rituals are dust . . . yet one alone,
Soul sister to the whippoorwill & crow,
Still wanders here. Still feels the star-winds blow
From distant space where chaos keeps its throne.

These columns hold no mysteries for she
Who traced their patterns from her freshest days
To final twilight shredding like a veil
Between the Ones who were—*are still to be*—
& summerlings whose lives must fade away
Before the sovereignty of sharper gales.

Climate of Fear

There is a wind made terrible by time
That rages through the raw Antarctic wastes;
Its voice near human, hideous with rhyme,
Suggestive of a species Man replaced
Too early & too utterly to mark
Its myth as more than whispers from the dark.

The sea-ice of the shoreline knows its force,
Likewise the islands only seals frequent;
Yet certain seasons signify its course
Between those haunted peaks that represent
A barrier best left in mystery
By all who crave a longer history.

What waits beyond is ancient past our kind's
Brief reckoning. Cyclopean & vast,
Its labyrinthine form reflects no mind
Arisen from the apes who shaped our past:
A citadel, instead, for spawn of stars
Light-years & lightless dreams away from ours.

Down countless corridors worn slick as glass,
Each wall inscribed in sinister detail
Depicting times no nightmare could surpass—
Strange battles, dire defeats—the wind exhales
With temperatures far less of Earth than void,
Securing both destroyer & destroyed.

Thus it has been for aeons. Sleep is death
Enough, if cold enough, to hold such things;
Yet recently some ape-corrupted breath
Of warmth has twisted through this gale . . . & brings
Dread dreams of waking to abyssal pools
Where formless horror mocks at nature's rules.

Some blighted day, when more than dreams arise
Released by fatal change to claim our place,
What stratagem, what desperate surmise,
Can save us? Or must we become a race
Emblazoned with extinction's bleak device—
Not from the stars turned right, but from the ice?

Weird of the White Sybil

You see me as you wish, a lissome maid
Descended from some lunar race of old,
& never dream that you should be afraid.

No matter that my draperies are frayed
By tempests only glacial wastelands hold.
You see me as you wish, a lissome maid

Less prophetess than purest spirit strayed
From paradise—or legends left untold—
& never dream that you should be afraid

To follow in my footsteps. Undismayed
As any moth hypnotic flames enfold,
You see me as you wish: a lissome maid

Who flickers at your vision's edge, displayed
Within a bower, brilliant in the cold.
O, never dream that you should be afraid

To speak your love . . . or to embrace its shade
As one more of the fortune-favored bold
Who saw me as a wish, a lissome maid
To kiss their dreams. *Too late to be afraid.*

—after Clark Ashton Smith

Yhoundeh Fades

Her inquisition chambers wait
In vain. Too silent, now; too clean,
Exquisite blades & pain-machines
Teach no more innocents the fate
Of heresy. The high priest's gate
Sags webbed in ebon silk, pristine
As dust upon his chalice green
With verdigris & mithridate.

Throughout the fanes of Mu Thulan
A strange & bitter incense burns
Once more to desecrate its sky
With daemon-rites not meant for man,
Unless to herald the return
Of Him who squats in dim N' kai.

—*after Clark Ashton Smith*

To the Next Priest

Barbarians, you call us, heretics
Who sacrifice the sanctity of death
On superstition's altar. With our sticks
& stones, we fracture ribs & stop the breath
Once more to anchor our ancestral dead
Past restlessness—or that undying thirst
No grave constrains. Nor prayer. Good words said
Make no more difference than the very worst
At moonrise on that third night after. Come,
Keep watch with us. The freshest mounds crack wide
Enough to show—almost—what strains inside
Against our sharpened staves & break-jaw bricks
Rammed home with love. Shriek till your throat bleeds numb,
& see then if you call us heretics.

Torn Out

It is dangerous to sleep here, and forbidden. Here in winter's depths, when twilight bleeds like a bruise into afternoon and the air is weighted with warm dust, the librarians begin their patrols early. Soft-voiced and hard-eyed, they rouse drowsy readers of magazines. Benumbed users of computer terminals. Questing deep in the stacks, they seek out the drab parka cocoons of the homeless, harrying them away with rumors of police.

> closing door
> a whisper in the vein
> fades

Only those who have worked among books for a long time comprehend these faces. Strange and pale, thirsting for a past which is their present—their future—they are called by the twin lures of literature and easy prey. Always there will be comfortable chairs in obscure corners. Always there will be some who do not wake. This place stands open to all, its guardians betrayed by anemic budgets and municipal codes.

> the cost
> by morning light
> stained pages

Mardi Gras Postmortem

There's jugular jazz in the Quarter tonight,
& the moon's gone missing. On Bourbon Street,
late revelers' throats arch taut & sweet
in the shadow land between streetlights
where lost souls watch . . . .yet mocking krewes
who scatter beads to the mob suspect
no threat behind gilt masks, detect
no thirst past Beaujolais & blues.

Come Lenten dawn, when sweepers rise
to curse their thankless task ahead,
they'll find amid the other trash
a sight to baffle bloodshot eyes:
more empties, torn & spattered red,
with rictus masks as pale as ash.

Desert Protocol

What blooms
bears thorns.

What howls
hears moon.

What lurks
endures.

What flees
is meat.

What dies
shall rise.

Flash Specters

The blast that claimed us came too quick. Burned free
of flesh & life alike, our spirits hold
to shadow as the last reality.

Past hunger or despair, past heat or cold,
our needs are nothing now . . . or just begun
in darkness that allows us to unfold

unfettered from the tyranny of sun
outlining us against our ravaged walls
forever in an instant. Overrun

from overhead, we never heard the call
to shelter, never felt the sirens wail
between our bones—& so each evening falls

upon us like a liberation. Veiled
in plainest sight, we haunt an enemy
who cannot comprehend of conquest failed,

or gaining nothing by a victory
too instant to allow us peaceably
to leave. To die. To let our vengeance be.

Time Ghosts

Our times call ghosts to us. Though Homer knew
the power of dark blood to loosen tongues
parched centuries past silence, we insist
on sensory amnesia when the same
shades permeate the wreck of Port-au-Prince
with Pompeii's wailings. While the limbless wraiths
who stalk Rwanda mourn their martyring
in Cathar accents, or some murdered girl
misnames her honor killing as *sati,*
we disbelieve . . . as if coincidence
alone explained such wounds of history
reopening afresh to slake a thirst
familiar as the ghosts of our bad nights,
& like them wandering unsatisfied
between hells happening that no one meant.

Towers of Light

They burn all night at the edges of our vision, luminescent as nuclear fungi. Translucent as tears. Darkness slides from their heights to drown our tattered lives, and we welcome its blindness.

Behind those spidered panes leaking heat into winter's infinity—rimed with ice far purer than the snows blistering our lips—shadows dance and mock and swirl. Untouchable in their towers of light, they stalk Möbius corridors where imagination failed. The inevitable unthinkable. We inhabit its cratered remains, not daring to gaze up. Our own faces in shadow.

> half-lives
> the brightness of
> decay

Frost Ghosts

Their scent is lilac, mostly. Caught
like blossoms martyred by a freeze
too late in April, their unease
at being dead at all comes fraught
with strange illusions. Knot by knot
they fall undone. A venomed breeze
exhales them: pale things like disease
imagined briefly, battles fought
in distant nations . . . . visions weak
as watered dreams, & yet we breathe
them eagerly, rejecting air
less tainted. Tempted by the bleak
allure of Aprils lost, we sheathe
our minds in lilac-sweet despair.

Wind Shift

In autumn, the leaves grow heavy with omens
cryptic & golden, poisoned & red
as stepmother's apples. Edged with light
already tilting overhead,

already weighted toward the grave,
they flutter like the tongues of masks
about to drop. What lies beneath
may wait in silence & unasked

another year. Or not. Such shades
as these distract our dreaming minds
from darkness & the earth stripped clear
of consequence. Yet still behind

these burning visions, twilight slips
inexorably. Broken seals
which once secured our blindness leave
the twisted bones of things revealed.

The Night of Her Return

Chill winds at midnight ripple cloth of gold:
these draperies whose twisted arabesques
suggest no single form, yet somehow hold
a thousand shadows of the pure grotesque.
I watch in vain, for none recall to me
the shadow of my love who ceased to be.

Sarcophagi from Luxor's sacred sites
transform the obscure angles of this room
with auguries of life eternal, rites
assuring swift deliverance from the tomb.
I curse them all. No ancient god, no power,
spared my Ligeia in her final hour.

Yet now a thread of scented vapor seeping
down from that censer whose strange-colored fires
conjured a shade to rouse my soul from sleeping
rekindles certain memories & desires
so vividly, I almost seem to hear
the whisper of her breath upon my ear.

Imagination? Madness? Opium?
All three, I fear . . . until another gasp
from what was once a deathbed turns me numb
to all but marvels promised in the past
by one who struggled (*might be struggling still?*)
against death's tyranny with love & will.

These cerements which bind the weak blonde clay
of her successor, what do they conceal?
My trembling fingers seek, then shrink away
from joys too terrible to be revealed:
the twining midnight masses of her hair,
her wild black eyes—and that triumphant stare.

—*after E. A. Poe's "Ligeia"*

Medusa, Becoming

Given myself as an unasked weapon,
I fled from Her temple broken & whole,
neither maid nor merely woman,

a shattered innocence consoled
by venom. Hissings from my hair
sent conversations twining cold

between my vertebrae, & where
I walked, small birds fell silent. Fell
like apples rotting. Undeclared

war echoed from my step: each swell
of hip or thigh or half-clad breast
thrust forth defiance, though I held

myself still victim. Past protest
or remedy, my belly sparked
with flutterings of white-winged death,

I sought my changed reflection—marked
it briefly in a young man's eyes—
& watched it wane to polished dark

harmless as pebbles. Wounded wise,
I reached out softly. Plucked my prize.

Goodnight Aileen

Some broken things don't heal. The highway takes
them young & as it finds them: no regrets,
no questions, no demands. Its silence lets
them fantasize that even last mistakes
can be outrun—that motion is salvation
granted at gunpoint. Gangrene of the soul
sets in & spreads, eroding self-control
to shadows fainter than imagination.

Half a dozen corpses later, fate
brings down this prey turned predator at last.
Long silence ended, she defies all slings
& arrows, rolls her sleeves up, & awaits
the chemical excision of her past,
the certainty of healing broken things.

*—Aileen Wuornos was executed by lethal injection at the
Florida State Prison on October 9, 2002.*

Keziah

". . . and who can say what underlies the old tales of broomstick
rides through the night?"

—H. P. Lovecraft, "The Dreams in the Witch House"

I. How It Began

She knew no God. The Devil, very well:
From every neighbor's narrowed prying eyes
A hint of brimstone shone. No further hell
Required for any woman grown too wise
With age, too solitary, & too poor
For much regard or grudging charity
Dispensed by goodwives from their kitchen doors,
With hissings to depart & leave them be.

No humble supplicant, she muttered dark
Beneath her breath as speculation spread
From tongue to idle tongue that she was marked
By witchery. Such superstitious dread
Excused their cruelty—or so they claimed—
Till she put nameless power to that name.

II. The White Stone

None living knew its origins. A stone
As leprous as the moon of some lost world,
It rose against the dark like vengeance hurled
From utter Void. She came to it alone
As seekers must, dream-driven to pursue
Deliverance by means beyond the pale
Provisioning of nature, & prevail
Against her enemies, though hell ensued.

Her answer slipped like shadow through the face
Of that great stone: a stranger robed in night
Itself, yet blacker still. He held a book
Filled with malignant magicks, time & space
Alike defiled . . . & as he bade her write
Her name in blood within, the heavens shook.

III. Nahab

Constrained no longer by the laws of man,
She wandered as she willed, & what she wrought
On certain Sabbats would not be forgot
In Arkham town for centuries. Tales ran
From house to house of horrors scarcely fit
For whispering: a missing infant's cry
Cut short in shadows, cattle bled out dry
By needle teeth. Half frightened from their wits,
Her neighbors sent to Salem. Strangers came
With sacred texts, & weapons freshly blessed
To search their alleys for a witch's nest—
Yet when they battered down her attic door,
A clamoring of witnesses proclaimed
What lay beyond was nothing seen before.

IV. Under Pressure

She told old Hathorne everything, at last:
The hideous fragility of space
Diaphanous as mist, through which she passed
Upon the Black Man's errands. Any place
Might open on a coven, & each rite
Conceal within its crude simplicity
Some undertone of Chaos, put to flight
Delusions of divine felicity . . .

He never let her finish. Proudly blind,
He prattled on about the Tempter's wiles,
So fatal to a weak & female mind.
His prisoner spat blood at him—then smiled,
Appearing not to notice when he said
She'd hang at cock-crow, by the neck, till dead.

V. Through Certain Angles

In blood lies power. By this primal law,
Mere curves & angles daubed on stone became
A well-mapped passage through our mundane frame
Of space to points *outside*. Those poisoned claws
Called justice could not touch her as she slipped
Between dimension-gates to heed the call
Pulsating out from that abyss where all
Persuasions & equations lose their grip
Upon reality. At length, a shrill
& mindless piping rose; yet as she knelt
Before her daemon-sultan on His throne
Of shattered stars, He knew her not until
She offered up her secret name—& felt
Herself delivered, chosen as His own.

VI. Of What Remained

They came for her at dawn, but found that cell
As empty as their understanding. Smeared
On every surface, figures rose & fell
Through ruptured space: the calculus of fear
Laid forth in gore. Her gaoler stayed behind
A fatal moment longer—till one heap
Of straw disclosed the ruin of his mind,
Likewise all reasoned speech or peaceful sleep.

Whatever scuttled from that fetid bed
Was neither rat, nor mouse, nor any beast
Begotten on this planet. Nightmare-bred,
It glared up from its interrupted feast
Amid a charnel-heap of splintered bones,
& cursed his soul to hell . . . in human tones.

The Queen's Speech

My daughters gone before me to the dark,
Dynastic sacrifices for a truth
Unbearable without this stranger's mask
That mocks me with its pallor—was his Sign
Sent forth for you at last, two maids in yellow
Awaiting the embrace of their dread king?

Carcosa's husk, a court without a king,
Lies echoing & hollow save for dark
Fumes rising from these guttered tapers. Yellow
No more with wholesome light, they died for truth
Made manifest among us by a sign
Denying life to all who dare unmask.

The voices of the Hyades still mask
My soul's lost song, unsung for any king
Save he who comes, the sender & the Sign
Combined at last. Ring down this final dark
To round our play of ages in a truth
Bitter past bearing, venomous & yellow!

Our Dynasty has borne a taint of yellow
Since Demhe's clouded depths lay clear, unmasked
Beneath the raw black stars. This phantom truth
Divides us from all others, save that king
Whose tattered mantle beckons from the dark
To each inheritor of his bleak Sign.

So many aeons passed without a sign
To guide us as Carcosa's towers yellowed
From leprous marble shining in that dark
Behind the moon, till madness like a mask
Of saffron veiled us from ourselves. O King,
When I am dead, what tongue shall sing this truth?

Perhaps no living eye can know such truth
As Hali's cloud-waves hid. Perhaps no sign
Is sent, but only shadows of a king
Lengthening like men's thoughts, strange & yellow
Across this hall where I alone, unmasked,
Retrace my daughters' footsteps into dark.

These eyes behold one final truth writ yellow:
Carcosa's doom, a sign all mortal masks
Lie fallen to that King beyond the dark.

—*after Robert W. Chambers*

At the Last of Carcosa

Peel back the mask of truth, that pallid skin
half phantom at our feast, half masquerade
against futility. As night begins
its metamorphosis from fleeting shade
to entropy, our city grows afraid
of faces & their machinations. Best
to pass in silence—every specter laid
by tattered saffron mystery; the rest
of us in waiting. Kindled black stars test
the firmness of a firmament long drained
to ashen dregs, & soul-songs die unblessed
beneath strange moons. No certainty remains
beyond one truth still worthy of the name:
unmasked at last, our skulls are all the same.

—after Robert W. Chambers

Outside the Chamber

(Washington Square, April 1920)

The line begins at dusk, as shadows drift
Between the gilded railings of that square
Few seek by day, in hopes of finding there
Despair's surcease. Secured like some great gift
Or mystery, oblivion awaits;
Its cloud-waves breaking over distant shores
& shadows of men's thoughts, while ever more
These waiting ones take on the shade of Fate.

In darkness filled with furtive murmuring
None but the self-condemned may understand,
They speak of matters spectral & malign:
Hastur, Aldebaran, a tattered King
Returned triumphant . . . & in every hand,
The fatal visitation of his Sign.

—after Robert W. Chambers

Finale, Act Two

The ebon snows have drifted deep
Along the shoreline of Hali
Assuring that dynastic sleep

Which ever was, shall ever be
The fate of kings whose samite masks
Veil little more than entropy

Incarnate in the blood. Unasked,
They ruled by runes they dared not name
Until a jaundiced phantom tasked

Their line with sorcery. That shame
They tasted once as mortals fled
Before a greater Sign which came

Eclipsing foes like twin suns bled
To ash behind their moons. Unslaked
By any wine save life, it fed

Until Carcosa's towers quaked
& shattered past redemption. Dust
Engulfed the stars as shadows waked

In Demhe's clouded depths, & rust
Of aeons claimed that coronet
Once called the Hyades. Upthrust

Against the void, things men forget
In waking out of nightmare cried
With one dark voice—*Hastur!*—& yet

A tattered wind alone replied
In threnodies through bones which keep
Bleak vigil where Cassilda died

Beneath those snows still drifting deep,
Along a shore where cloud-waves creep
Into their sorceries of sleep.

—after Robert W. Chambers

The Winds of Sesqua Valley

The winds of Sesqua Valley sigh tonight
Among the leaves of cemetery trees,
Whose roots reclaim each wanderer by right
Of that dark heartbeat pulsing like a sea
Beneath the shadow-spell of Selta's glance
As trueborn children gather for the dance.

Meanwhile, one exiled spirit lost among
The echoes of a world grown too mundane
To hear beyond itself awaits—in vain—
His summons home. A summoning unsung
By all but dying stars above that tower
Where Sesqua's hierophant sequesters power.

The winds of Sesqua Valley cry tonight
From Selta's summit . . . or some outer place
Untouched & uncorrupted by the light
Of our raw spark. Swept round by this embrace,
Each dancer's steps delineate a Sign
In equal parts infernal & divine.

Against a void grown leprous with the glow
Of mortal lives, an exile lifts his hand
In answer—though the last who understand
Departed from this wasteland long ago,
To dwell instead beneath primeval skies,
Adoring Khroyd'hon with their argent eyes.

The winds of Sesqua Valley die tonight,
Dismissing those who wove their threnody
With foot & flute to speed the failing might
Of all mankind has been, or hopes to be.
Elsewhere, a dreamer exiled from their ways
Takes up his pen of ebony, & plays.

—for W. H. Pugmire

Of One Who Dreamed

The old gods wake! From pole to pole, that cry
Disquiets midnight in a thousand tongues
Both common & unknown to prophesy
Some cataclysm. Since this world was young,
Its gods have come & gone; their praises sung
In temples or in battle, their rites kept
With incense or with sacrifice fresh-wrung
From writhing flesh. Yet elder powers slept
Beneath our seas. Beyond our stars. Adept
At camouflage, they shaped the waking dreams
Of one whose bleak imagination leapt
To correlate its contents—into reams
Of warning left behind for all who sense
The stirrings of a darker Providence.

Gone to Ground

There is no turning from the hounds of Time,
No victory. In going swift to ground
& burrowing through leaf-mold streaked with slime,
There is no turning. From the hounds of Time
A baying rises, signifying crime
& punishment made one: your gravesite found,
There is no turning. From the hounds of Time,
No victory in going swift to ground.

Ammutseba Rising

At first, a spectral haze against the darkness,
some apparition less of mist than hunger
made visible afflicts our evening. Stars
within it flicker, fettered by corruption
we sense but dimly. Terrible & ancient,
it murmurs in the dreams of chosen daughters.

Not *it*, but *She* . . . Chaos Incarnate's daughter
thought-spawned at random from that primal darkness
past memory or myth returns. What ancient
sorceries survive to wake such hunger
in times like ours? What spirit of corruption
endures to threaten these well-charted stars?

Minds blind to science, doubtful of the stars,
accustomed to dominion over daughters
& wives alike defy this world's corruption
with ignorance. No curse, but blessed darkness
obscuring every sin—or any hunger
for truth beyond the authorized & ancient.

Above us now, authority more ancient
than mankind manifests. As fading stars
surrender up their essence to a hunger
yet unsuspected by our science, daughters
of ignorance awake. Unveiled from darkness,
they lift their faces. Savor sweet corruption.

Arched like a crime-scene silhouette, corruption
assumes the form of female. Feral. Ancient
opener of all the ways to darkness,
Her mystery eclipses tarnished stars
we kept for wishing on. Perhaps our daughters
will walk in shadow gladly, holding hunger

inside them for a weapon. Nameless hunger
reshaped their spirits: should we fear corruption
in doing likewise? All of us are daughters
denied some truth or other; craving ancient
wisdom like the bitterness of stars
against Her tongue, expiring into darkness.

No dawn remains. O daughters called by ancient
hunger, know the truth of your corruption:
Devourer of Stars, perfected darkness.

The *Ba*-Curse

They asked him if he feared the mummy's curse,
That blameless maid he'd stolen from her tomb.
The excavator laughed: he'd heard far worse
In every local *souk*. As twilight's gloom
Suffused the valley like the Nile at flood,
He lit a lamp & tied his tent-flaps tight,
Then with a flourish fit to freeze the blood,
He poured a dram & bade his prize good night.

They never knew what savaged him, although
He shrieked it very clearly as he died:
"*Ba*! *Ba*!" A madman's babble . . . even so,
His men won't speak of things they saw inside,
For neither time nor whiskey can erase
That black-winged nightmare with a maiden's face.

Horizon of the Aten

(for the commoner dead of Amarna)

This place was free of gods before we came
To build a god on earth his bleak desire:
A virgin altar for the Aten's fire
That seared his mind. We spoke the sacred names
Of Thebes too seldom here. Ground down like grain
We rarely tasted, silence was our lot,
Although the sun-disk's prophet soon forgot
Our lives entirely. Profits of our pain
Laid out in faience, gardens, palace stones
In ordered rows endured, but flesh was sand
Upon the wind's tongue scouring this land
Past gods. Or visions. Or a lost king's throne.

Our *ba*s are starveling, broken-pinioned things
Like sparrows bickering around our graves
For scraps of prayer. In life & death undone
Not by a rising, but a sinking sun,
We cling to its horizon—though it saved
Us from the gods no better than these wings.

Set Comes to Whitechapel

He speaks in hieroglyphs of red
no modern priest may understand,
strange wisdom from a god long dead.

From lightless street to frightful bed,
Chaos incarnate haunts the land.
He speaks in hieroglyphs of red,

relating how his hunger fed
on flaunting prey too close to hand:
strange wisdom, from a god. Long dead,

& yet such mysteries embed
themselves in flesh. With every strand,
he speaks in hieroglyphs of red

things rising from men's hearts—or bred
by want's unalterable demands,
strange wisdom. From a god long dead,

the future draws its crimson thread
across our throats. Unsought, unplanned,
it speaks in hieroglyphs of red,
strange wisdom from a god long dead.

Eating Mummy

The dust of dynasties upon my lips
Drifts bitter as a natron kiss. Like breath
Long centuries unsweetened by the tomb,
Its tang is death.

Torn from a simpler immortality,
This soul was body, now forever lost
Between the teeth of one whose ignorance
Saw little cost.

Cast by a failing candle I dare not
Extinguish yet—or ever—shadows crawl
In hieroglyphs of prophecy across
My sickroom wall.

What promises apothecaries lied
To lighten weighted hearts fall into sleep
Grown turbulent & troubled as the Nile
At dog star deep.

No feather calms these waters. Ripples rise
Instead from snout & scale & ripsaw teeth
Half visible, half mythic as the bulk
Of beast beneath.

Devourer of souls! No ignorance
Runs deep enough to drown this certainty
Fresh-clawed into the cringing heart of one
Unfit to be.

Awakened into judgment, I behold
My shadow altered. Superstition's pawn,
Devourer I was—& shall be known
From this night on.

Night Laundry

(London, 1843)

It's all to do with pounds & pence: the rest
Is sentiment the poor can ill afford
When death itself presents the final test
Of slender means. To take a stranger's word
Comes hard—but, ah, his coin's another thing
Entirely when a man's got babes to feed,
& her who bore them lying cold. *Just bring*
That basket of yours round, sir. Yes, indeed,
It's for the best. At least she'll have a grave
When all is . . . done, & none need ever know,
Especially her Da who slaved & saved
To send her here from Derry years ago.

The wail of laden wheels soon fades away
In gas-lit fog, rejoining other carts
Heaped innocent with linen for the day's
Deliveries around the back at Barts,
Where some who took in laundry all their lives
Are taken in themselves, for students' knives.

Kingdom of the Spirits

(Asmat)

In this kingdom of the spirits, men are trees.
The sago teaches where their fruit is found
& hints at harvest: how to seize the seed
of life, renaming new men out of youth.

The sago teaches where that fruit is found
atop the trunk, above its branches' grasp
of life. Renaming new men out of youth
requires a reach—the spirit of a spear

atop the trunk, above its branches' grasp
at sap already flowing from the thrust
required. The reach. The spirit of a spear
as sure as crocodile or mantis thirsting

at sap already flowing from the thrust
that claims a name. Now all the rest is carving
as sure as crocodile or mantis thirsting
upon a pole of ancestors entwined

with claims & names. Now all the rest is carving
to free the fruit for use, & leave its sap
upon a pole where ancestors entwine
awaiting vengeance: warriors who seek

to free more fruit for use. To leave fresh sap
on other poles, appeasing other spirits
awaiting vengeance-warriors who seek
at last Safan, the land beyond the sea,

on other poles. Appeasing other spirits
with their own jawless rinds bereft of pulp
at last. Safan, the land beyond the sea,
holds ancestors past memory who howl

(despite their jawless rinds bereft of pulp)
in death. Disease. *Tuans* with guns, whose laws
hold ancestors past memory . . . who howl
like children at the wisdom of a spear

hinting at harvest: how we seize the seed
in this kingdom of the spirits. Men are trees.

Last Light, Frijoles Canyon

(Bandelier National Monument)

Time falls away with twilight in this place
Where cavates with their death's-head hollow stare
Return the gaze of stragglers who dare
Remain behind at closing—dare to face
Emerging bats who swarm on spectral wings
Like spirits out of torment from these walls
Incised with nightmare. Nameless shadows crawl
Across the earth till only ladders bring
Deliverance, & from some shallow scrape,
A view best left to silence. Language holds
No virtue in the face of strangeness old
As Earth's first masters: wiser to escape
Than witness as a wounded sunset dies
What horrors came to make men dig so high.

Desert Nocturne

The sun is young here, but each night
falls ancient as the curse of Cain
upon a land that murders sight
in canyon shadows. Where the rains
of eons murmured their refrain
until the ravaged earth gave way
by layers, chaos written plain
in fossil glyphs too strange for day
emerges—& this troubled clay
surrendering to sunset hides
its soul no longer. Mortal gray
becomes the indigo of tides
where entities no man has known
awake to claim us for their own.

—in memoriam Adam Niswander

Fiesta of Our Lady

Another dusty chile-growing town
Just off the highway in New Mexico,
With banners, flags, & streamers hanging down
To brighten streets where weekend tourists go . . .
Yet ancient, alien malevolence
Twists through this scene of rural innocence.

Though every booth & table in the square
Entreats Our Lady's favor on this day
Of celebration, few outsiders care
To question further. Locals glance away,
Or offer a *cervaza*—Ice cold! Free!—
In hopes the curious will let things be.

Some few, alas, do not. As afternoon
Wears on into a raggedy parade
Which manifests no sign of ending soon,
These unwise souls go seeking after shade
Down narrow streets where shadows twine & snake,
Luring them onward to their last mistake.

A low adobe chapel wedged between
Two buildings lost already to the earth
Seems quaint enough—until the altar screen,
Adorned with serpent-shapes whose length & girth
Suggest some mythic origin. Outside,
The throb of drums begins. But where to hide?

Before the altar, one tile out of place
Reveals a glimpse of darkness echoing
Off rough-carved stairs descending into space
Which stinks of primal musk. Though everything
Of reason rules against it, still those drums
Spark horror in their hindbrains. Down they come.

What waits below is older than Man's dreams
Of deity in his own image. Here
Within this cavern sanctified by screams
& sacrifice for generations, fear
Assumes a shape instinctively profane—
A writhing, hissing insult to the brain.

Past other totem animals of faith,
The serpent grips imagination tight
Within its coils: thus Yig, dread father-wraith
Of rattlesnakes who haunts the desert night—
& shadowing that presence, She who bore
Him & his demon siblings by the score.

The azure atmosphere of deep K'n-Yan
First held the mysteries of Her worship, while
This young world harbored other lords than man:
Star-spawned abominations, strange & vile,
Who voyaged deathless through the vacuum seas
To spread their stain on our mythologies.

Struck suddenly aghast before Her form
Whose twin mouths gape with venom & desire,
The interlopers (too late!) hear a swarm
Of devotees descending, bearing fire
& sharp obsidian to spill that wine
Most suited to Our Lady's dark design.

Another sleepy chile-growing town
Just off the highway in New Mexico,
But now these precious fields lie green, not brown,
Beneath the sun. Best tourists never know
The secret of this land's fertility . . .
O Serpent-Skirted One Who Should Not Be!

Mother's Night

May moonlight lends these waves a spectral glow
Akin to phosphorescence fathoms down
Beyond a dark reef only locals know
Which haunts the harbor-mouth of Innsmouth town.
One night each year, a shambling, shadowed horde
Assembles on the cobbles of this shore
To crouch in silence, faces turning toward
Those depths where ceremonies long before
Brought forth a strange deliverance—or bane—
To mark their blood forever. Siblings all,
They wait for Her on whom their fathers called,
& glory in the knowledge of Her reign
Beneath immortal seas . . . where Her embrace
Shall welcome every child of Hydra's race.

Lullaby for Arachnophobes

Remember, children: spiders never sleep.
Conspicuous among the attic beams,
Their webs stretch wide; & what they catch, they keep.

Some drift on silken chutes. Some even leap
Upon their prey to suffocate their screams.
Remember, children: spiders never sleep—

Their eyes are multiple, their thoughts are deep
Beyond the boundaries of human schemes.
Their webs stretch wide; & what they catch, they keep

Wrapped mummy-tight. You'd never make a peep
Although your bones were softening to cream.
Remember, children: spiders never sleep

The way we do, which gives them time to creep
Inside our drowsy minds in search of dreams.
Their webs stretch wide; & what they catch, they keep

No matter how it struggles or it weeps . . .
So please don't. It's much later than it seems.
Remember, children: spiders never sleep.
Their webs stretch wide; & what they catch, they keep.

Blown Out

There are five this year. No two from the same roadside stand. Selected for some resemblance only his knife recognizes, each awaits that first stab of metal into flesh. He takes his time. Reaching in with twisted fingers, he splats handfuls onto yesterday's news until all five stand hollow as his heart.

> hunter's moon
> the last crescent
> sharpest

Unwrapping the last candle, he cups it in his hands, inhaling deeply. The scent holds grave-mold and brimstone, raven's brains and blood copper. A sheen of grease. In the bayou where he obtained the candles decades ago, children often went missing. He settles the squat black cylinder into place and strikes a match.

> empty box
> fills with shadows
> spider silk

Eleven forty-nine. Spaced along the porch railing, his enemies' faces flicker and blaze in a fickle wind. Already he imagines each tiny fire extinguished. Each soul dismissed to the miseries it has earned. He will read tomorrow's paper with interest, sifting random tragedies for the five marks of his intention.

Eleven fifty-nine. His fingers tighten on a stem. Success equals details: one flame, one exhalation. Move on. Then move again—again—until the twelfth stroke, a final spiral of burnt flesh incense.

One. Two. Three. Four . . .

> sudden gust
> the night inside
> absolute

Wolves of Mars

We never thought about there being *two*.
Our moons, that is: the terror & the fear
Of their incessant chase on nights too clear
To turn away. This legend we pursue
Pursues us even here, defying shells
We built to shield us from ourselves at last,
Abandoning a planet's worth of past
In hopes of wiping out some future hell
We packed along.
                 Now every dawn is doubt
Of neighbor. Lover. Self. Whose eyes caught fire?
Whose tongue knew blood? Each question leaves a scar
Our night-pelts hide . . . until to go without
Becomes more dangerous than red desire,
Than proof we cannot wall out what we are.

Alexandria Next Time

They look nothing like us. We expect nothing: we are a research crew. To the god knowledge we long ago sacrificed preconceptions and perspectives. We see with eyes so altered as to be useless anywhere but at the bleeding edge. As the archivists scuttle towards us, we barely wonder what flesh fills those carapaces.

> the unrolled whisper
> of papyrus
> footfalls

One brush of our minds ignites their translation orbs' eloquence. They speak the wisdom of worlds past our most ambitious slip. Salvaged texts from empires perished before Sol's kindling, trans-dimensional logic inscribed within crystals which *phase*. Such is their custom, their sole requirement. The copyists await.

> salt tang
> lingers in the ink
> stained fingers

We offer up all the information we carry. Data banks, storage matrices, log compilations, even a few cherished hardbooks. Yet their orbs flicker disappointment—we are no new thing. All we have seen or heard, theorized or prophesized, is known from elsewhere.

Our bestbrightest huddle in desperation. Abruptly, one archivist turns. Orb blazing one moment, shadow-swirled the next, it muses upon unstable formats still possibly useful. Selecting three bestbrightest, it leads them from our ship.

starlit waves
the scroll racks fill
with silence

Their invitation comes five days later. Eager to learn what our absent colleagues have helped transcribe, we enter the great library at last. Spherical, chimerical, fantastic with webbed ladders and spun-metal chambers, it enshrines more knowledge than our worship has imagined. Where to begin?

In one new-minted room, archivists surround a transparent nutrient tank. Much waving of limbs: we are summoned. Its orb aglow, our guide presents our captain with three flat black cases. *Profound thanks . . . to preserve residual organics . . . not possible . . . fair copies provided . . .*

The unhinged carapace top reveals no flesh. Only a flat black case. And beyond it, three floating gray cauliflowers.

retracing
lost arc of history
torch spark

A Voyage(r) Too Far

It was not meant that we should voyage far,
Nor risk the limits of our sanity
Beyond the fragile light that marks our star.

All ignorant of where—& what—we are,
We launched twin probing blips of vanity.
It was not meant that we should voyage far,

Yet those black seas bewitched us like the tar
That took La Brea's beasts. Humanity,
Beyond the fragile light that marks our star,

May prove no more than fireflies in a jar
Against the mindless void: insanity
It was not meant that we should voyage far

Enough to taste. What dark god's avatar
Awaits our first breath of profanity
Beyond the fragile light that marks our star?

Dream-maddened poets know . . . & bear a scar
Of mind that shrieks His inhumanity.
It was not meant that we should voyage far
Beyond the fragile light that marks our star.

We live on a placid island of ignorance in the midst of black seas of
infinity, and it was not meant that we should voyage far.
—H. P. Lovecraft

Aurelia Aurita

The world ocean devours us. Night by wave it gnaws the pitted pillars of our last and highest cities, the acid of its own long dying seeping into our dreams. Our blood. Our tongues. We are fewer than we were, but too late and each alone. Narrow blind windows like haunted mirrors stare down from all sides, overlooking the gelatinous shadows of our inheritors as they thicken the waters further with their seed.

The patience of polyps, adrift through warm decades ahead.

Through the stars without us.

>   an instant
>   of translucence
>   rising moon

Of Pluto, P4, & Paranoia

It's not a planet nowadays. In fact,
We kicked it to the Kuiper curb to make
Some scientific point . . . or some mistake
Mankind might not survive. While we distract
Ourselves with definition, there remains
An aura of the ominous about
This lonely roller at the rim which shouts
In tones of panic to our primal brains.

Its very name holds nightmare—& three moons
Thus far, although a fourth lurks in the dark
Unlabeled. Unsuspected. Might some spark
Of prescience catch at last (& none too soon)
To grant the malediction it deserves,
Murmuring of *Yuggoth* to our nerves?

Void Music

Space is not silent, save for mundane ears
Attuned to flesh alone. The aether swells
With arias & whispers while we tell
Our tales of plasma waves, reshaping fear
As placid science. Island-dwellers cast
Adrift by proxy on a vast black sea
Should trust a little less in certainties
So fragile: did we voyage here unasked
Expecting welcome? Blind inside this drape
Of instruments, our curiosity
Expands as *hubris*, exponentially,
Athirst for evidence of our escape.

Meanwhile in undimensioned night beyond
Our sphere of ignorance, strange shadows drift
& sing the death of starlight. One by one,
Their threnodies thread ripples through this pond
Reality . . . until some chorus shifts
To sound the flickering of our brief sun.

Darkest Anodyne

Strange aeons are upon us. Madness lies
Too near the surface now, & nightmares creep
Beyond the subtle borderline of sleep
To taint our waking. Though we civilize
Perdition into pixels, wary eyes
Cannot deny the anarchy that seeps
Through every screen deployed in vain to keep
A hundred horrid truths unrealized.

What comfort on such nights to read, instead,
Of entities inhuman & obscure
Who claimed this planet once—& might again
If asked politely. Truly, Alhazred
Sang prophecy: his chronicler endures
As darkest anodyne against our pain.

—for the 78th anniversary of H. P. Lovecraft's passing

Afterword: A Medium Rare

How can this little book possibly accommodate so many worlds? Each successive page is a door into another one. Each poem comes packed with presupposed realities, fully present in a few lines. One might want to consider whether one wants to read several of them in a single setting, because that way lies jet-lag. Any one of the poems is liable to whisk you away like the demon in Lovecraft's *Fungi from Yuggoth*. Savor them, I say. Ankh (as I call her) did not write them in a single, frenetic blaze of glory, and they should not be read in a single spree. At least that's my advice.

Numerous ghosts drift through these pages, and some of them are readily recognizable and would be even if the poet did not openly acknowledge the fountains from which she drank. Like Scrooge encountering the seven-years-dead Jacob Marley, you may start in awe at tracing the familiar features of Poe, Lovecraft, Clark Ashton Smith, and Chambers, but you will in the same moment greet their surprising return with the fondness of old friends.

When I read her sonnets I can well believe Ankh is a medium channeling the Muse that spoke through HPL in his own supernatural sonnetry, so I am grateful to find a few specimens of that form here. But there is much else besides. Her poetic skills are on full display in these pages. It is easily possible at first to be swept up in her magic and only later to pause to examine the techniques of wizardry she has employed to such great advantage. The rhymes one scarcely notices at first because of the complete lack of contrivance, the effortless-seeming facility of plucking startlingly apt and uncommon metaphors as if the poet were a champion swimmer in a broad, deep sea of language. All reveals Ann K. Schwader as a mature and accomplished poet, one intimate with her Muse and obedient to her gentle leading.

Ankh has learned the secret that Gerard Genette teaches so well in his classic treatment, *The Architext*, namely that poetry creates its own self-contained world. The language of poetry is essentially *intransitive*. That is, a poem is not trying to communicate information. We have prose for that. Or, as Tom Ligotti says in "Vastarien," a poem is "not *about* a thing but simply *is* that thing." In Peter L. Berger's terms, a poem stands isolated and insulated as a "finite province of meaning" having little if anything to do with the outside, public world. Thus poetry is relieved of the challenge facing prose fiction, which must disguise itself among mundane allusions so as to lull the reader into an ultimately false sense of secure familiarity—until the trap is sprung. Lovecraft knew this and did the trick well. And he knew just as clearly what Genette and Schwader know: that the poem is its own self-contained world.

A different variety of magic is required, of course, to conjure a world in a few strokes as the poet does. The poem, notably the fantastic poem, is like a space ship abducting a previously earthbound denizen. She has the technology necessary for the job and she knows how to use it. Think of Doug Bradley's Cenobite character in *Hellraiser*: "We have such things to show you!" Or of Alma Mobley in *Ghost Story*: "I will take you places you have never been. I will show you things that you've never seen!"

That's our Ankh, Ann of Seven Gables. What Keziah Mason managed to do with exotic geometry, Ann Schwader does with "mere" words, magic indeed.

—ROBERT M. PRICE

June 25, 2015

Index of Titles and First Lines

Acknowledgments

"Alexandria Next Time" *Scifaikuest* #7.3 (2011).

"Alien Machines," *Star*Line* #34.1 (2011).

"Ammutseba Rising," *She Walks in Shadows*, ed. Silvia Moreno-Garcia and Paula R. Stiles (Innsmouth Free Press 2015).

"At the Last of Carcosa," *Spectral Realms* #2 (2015).

"Aurelia Aurita," *Star*Line* #34.3 (2011).

"The *Ba*-Curse," *Candle in the Attic Window,* ed. Silvia Moreno-Garcia and Paula R. Stiles (Innsmouth Free Press 2011).

"Blown Out," *Phantasmagorium* #1 (2011).x

"Climate of Fear," *Spectral Realms* #1 (2014).

"*Cordyceps zombii*," *Fungi,* ed. Orrin Grey and Silvia Moreno-Garcia (Innsmouth Free Press 2012).

"Darkest Anodyne," Necronomicon Providence event/ Facebook page (2015).

"Deconstructing Night," *Strange Horizons* (2001).

"Desert Nocturne," *Weird Fiction Review* #4 (2013).

"Desert Protocol," *inkscrawl* #3 (2012).

"Eating Mummy," *Weird Fiction Review* #4 (2013).

"Fatal Constellations," *Weird Fiction Review* #5 (2014).

"Fiesta of Our Lady," *Lovecraft eZine* #14 (2012).

"Finale, Act Two," *A Season in Carcosa*, ed. Joseph S. Pulver, Sr. (Miskatonic River Press 2012).

"Flash Specters," *Star*Line* #36.4 (2013).

"Frost Ghosts," *Weird Fiction Review* #5 (2014).

"Giving Up the Ghost," *Eye to the Telescope* #4 (2012).

"In This Brief Interval," *Future Lovecraft*, ed. Silvia Moreno-Garcia and Paula R. Stiles (Innsmouth Free Press 2011).

"The Laundrymen," *Spectral Realms* #1 (2014).

"Lavinia in Autumn," *Autumn Cthulhu*, ed. Mike Davis ([*Lovecraft eZine* Press] 2015).

"Lullaby For Arachnophobes," *Eye to the Telescope* #4 (2012).

"A Maid Betray'd," *Dark Starr* #3.3 (1988).

"Mardi Gras Postmortem," *Architectures of Night* (Dark Regions Press 2003).

"Medusa, Becoming," *Star*Line* #35.1 (2012).

"Mercy, Mercy," *Eye to the Telescope* #6 (2012).

"Mother's Night," *Horror for the Holidays*, ed. Scott David Aniolowski (Miskatonic River Press 2011).

"Night Laundry," *Dreams & Nightmares* #96 (2013).

"The Night of Her Return," *Speculon* (2001).

"Of One Who Dreamed," Necronomicon Providence *Newsletter* (2014).

"Of Pluto, P4, & Paranoia," *Cyaegha* #7 (2012).

"Outside the Chamber," *Cyaegha* #13 (2015).

"The Queen's Speech," *Lovecraft eZine* #30 (2014).

"Thoughts at the Passing Bell," *Penny Dreadful* #14 (2002).

"Time Ghosts," *Ideomancer* #14.1 (2010).

"Torn Out," *Mythic Delirium* #24 (2011).

"To the Next Priest," *HWA Horror Poetry Showcase* #1 (2014).

"Towers of Light," *Star*Line* #36.2 (2013).

"Void Music," *Spectral Realms* #2 (2015).

"A Voyage(r) Too Far," *Eye to the Telescope* #6 (2012).

"Weird of the White Sybil," *Deepest, Darkest Eden*, ed. by Cody Goodfellow (Miskatonic River Press 2013).

"Wind Shift," *Weird Fiction Review* #3 (2012).

"The Winds of Sesqua Valley," *Lovecraft eZine* #28 (2013).

"Wolves of Mars," *Eye to the Telescope* #6 (2012).

"Yhoundah Fades," *Deepest, Darkest Eden*, ed. by Cody Goodfellow (Miskatonic River Press 2013).

All other works are original to this collection.

Dark Energies by Ann K. Schwader.
(August 2015)
ISBN: 978-0-9943901-0-3 (illustrated hardcover) $25AU
ISBN: 978-0-9804625-1-7 (illustrated paperback) $14AU
ISBN: 978-0-9943901-1-0 (illustrated ebook) $10AU

OTHER PUBLICATIONS FROM P'REA PRESS

Richard L. Tierney: A Bibliographical Checklist by Charles Lovecraft.
(February 2008)
ISBN: 978-0-9804625-0-0 (paperback) $6AU

Spores from Sharnoth and Other Madnesses by Leigh Blackmore.
(September 2008; rev. rpt, August 2010, May 2013)
ISBN: 978-0-9804625-2-4 (paperback) $14AU

Emperors of Dreams: Some Notes on Weird Poetry by S. T. Joshi.
(November 2008)
ISBN: 978-0-9804625-3-1 (paperback) $14AU
ISBN: 978-0-9804625-4-8 (hardcover, out of print)

Savage Menace and Other Poems of Horror by Richard L. Tierney.
(April 2010)
ISBN: 978-0-9804625-5-5 (illustrated numbered hardcover) $30AU
ISBN: 978-0-9804625-6-2 (illustrated ebook) $10AU

The Land of Bad Dreams by Kyla Lee Ward.
(September 2011)
ISBN: 978-0-9804625-7-9 (illustrated paperback) $14AU

Avatars of Wizardry by George Sterling, Clark Ashton Smith, et al.
(November 2012)
ISBN: 978-0-9804625-8-6 (illustrated paperback) $14AU
ISBN: 978-0-9804625-9-3 (illustrated ebook) $10AU

P'REA PRESS

Publishes weird and fantastic poetry and non-fiction
c/−34 Osborne Road, Lane Cove, NSW, Australia 2066
Email: DannyL58@hotmail.com